Attention
All Typewriters

JASON CAMLOT

Attention
All Typewriters

LIVRES
DC
BOOKS

Cover illustration by J. W. Stewart.
Author photograph by Heather Pepper.
Book designed and typeset in Adobe Garamond Pro
and Myriad MM by Primeau & Barey, Montreal.

Printed and bound in Canada by AGMV Marquis.
Distributed by Lit DistCo.

Legal Deposit, Bibliothèque nationale du Québec
and the National Library of Canada, 3rd trimester, 2005.

Library and Archives Canada Cataloguing in Publication
Camlot, Jason, 1967-
Attention all typewriters / Jason Camlot.

Poems.
ISBN 0-919688-01-2 (pbk.)
ISBN 0-919688-02-0 (bound)
I. Title.
PS8555.A5238A9 2005   C811'.6   C2005-904370-9

For our publishing activities, DC Books gratefully
acknowledges the financial support of The Canada
Council for the Arts, of SODEC, and of the
Government of Canada through the Book Publishing
Industry Development Program (BPIDP).

**Canada Council   Conseil des Arts
for the Arts   du Canada**

*Société
de développement
des entreprises
culturelles*
Québec 🏵🏵

DC Books
950 Decarie, Box 662
Montreal, Quebec, H4L 4V9
www.dcbooks.ca

For Cory, Oscar and Nava

Contents

IV. Important Men

V. Quaker Oats

I. Bewildered

Bewildered Alexandrines

Dazed speechless baffled flabbergasted mazed misled
Dumbfounded struck rebounded rattled in the head

Blind muddled hit befuddled knocked floored blown-breathless
Strewn puzzled flipped bedazzled into nothingness

Agape bamboozled battered wrecked confuséd lost
Addled shook confounded fazed hazy horror-tossed

Dismayed forlorn spun whirling ruffled to the core
Thrown flustered "off" bothered perplexed looking for more

Shamed crushed embarrassed burnt cut reeling fucked
Staggering awed astounded woozy wonderstruck

Disgraced aghast disturbed astonished stupefied
Afraid left in the dark bewildered but alive

Bewildered

For Rob Allen

I know the voices dying with a dying fall
Beneath the music from a farther room.
So how should I presume?
T. S. Eliot, "The Love Song of J. Alfred Prufrock"

TOWNIE ARSON (Headline from the
    Kenyon Collegian, April 18th, 1974)–
And the brownstones
Went black as wet blackboards, black as
Toledo Machine and Tool
Co. black steel drop hammers,
Black as the burnt onion paper pages
Of English literature anthologies.
Like refugees of a frosh-week war,
Professors and freshmen alike
Bore rescued parcels and treasures–
Notebooks, desk lamps, bedding and bongs–
To classrooms vacated for our new residency.
By lottery I won a Childhood
Education Observation Room
With a one-way mirror view of the John
Crowe Ransom terrarium, one door over;
The door marked, Therapy Room.

Who is this John Crowe Ransom,
New dorm-fellow of mine?
My best college buds,
Mooshoo and Grubmonkey,
Want to know since they now sleep
On my floor (declining the gym cots

They have won in the lottery.)
I find out from a fellow Kenyonite's
Term paper acquired through the
Kenyon Intelligence Secret Service (known as KISS,
But even more familiarly known as:
Kenyonites-Share-Essays-For-Money-Drugs-Or-Sex-Jobs.)
The essay I acquire, for one weed-roach and a worn paperback
Copy of *Thus Spake Zarathustra,*
Entitled, "John Crowe Ransom:
Our Living Kenyon College Treasure,"
Begins:

"Professor Ransom, born April 30th, 1888
In Pulaski, Tennessee, was the son
Of a strongly religious but also very open-minded
Methodist minister. The precocious young J.C.
Wrote his first hymn, and then immediately
Sang it by heart, at age three, entered Vanderbilt
University at age 15 and graduated in much less time
Than it usually takes. For several years he was
A Rhodes Scholar at Oxford, England.
[FOOTNOTE: Not to be confused with Oxford,
Mississippi, where another important man
Of American letters, William Faulkner, moved
To live at age five, and was, to our astonishment,
A mediocre student, and thereafter dropped out
Of high school in the tenth grade.]
After Rhodes, Professor J. C. Ransom taught
At Vanderbilt, his *Alma Mater* (which means

Fostering Mothers in the original Roman language.)
Then, in 1937, Professor J.C. departed for our very own
Kenyon College, where he has enriched our
Intellectual life ever since. Seventeen years
Before that momentous event, he married,
And with the aid of his wife
Had three children. Following his retirement
From teaching, and from editing the world-famous
Kenyon Review, in 1957, he stayed active
And continued to revise his early poems,
Most of which he wrote many years before,
When he was just a lad."

Thanks, Marcus Kevin Fifes, Sophomore, Majoring
In English with a Minor in Business Ethics.

Now, from my perspective adjacent to the once-
Precocious, now precariously-living,
I add to the biography: Toward the end
Of his life, John Crow Ransom suffered
From a variety of invisible things
That led him into long periods of withdrawal,
Silence, and unmotivated television watching.
On other occasions, he could be seen and heard
Carrying on lengthy conversations
With the fabulous spectres, unreal roommates,
Chimerical creatures of his glass-bound Imaginarium.

This is our story.

Actually, I just added that for dramatic effect.

But I do have something to offer
About this man in his final year,
Having watched his worn televisioned eyes,
Overheard his old Bakelite radio voice
Speak scenes from a life story in cryptograms
To invisible friends,
While I passed spliffs,
Or hash on a pin–
Little smoldering tears in the Viet Cong continuum–
Between my own friends,
More visible, arguably more real.

We shared a glassy room,
We listened to our tunes,
We measured out our months with *National Lampoons.*

Stupid Issue. May 1974.

"Why doesn't he change the channel?"
Grubsy's disturbed by J.C.'s televisionary apathy.
It was NBC Sunday night family hour.
"If he keeps this up,
He will remain indefinitely
The last of his kind," Moo haikus.
We three, Grubsy, Moo, and me,
Met last semester in the poetry workshop
Of hot-shot, itinerant Cornell
Neo-Romantic Carpe-Diemite, Professor REN.
REN had rent our minds asunder, and now
We too were Neo-Carpe-Romantic-Diemites,

Seizing our days away
In wafts of smoke
And Marvin Gaye,
In "Yo' Mamma Jokes"
And epitaph play.
We observe now
The arm-chaired Porcupine,
Light from the Zenith bending as
Glass thorns from his skull,
The quills of his *Annus Mirabilis*
Quivering with slight memory
As soft-bellied critters gather around him.
Suddenly,
Like a blackout ended,
Lazyboy dragonweight moves alive,
Voice box buzzing like those helicopters
From the third channel. He speaks
With precision through a reception
Of blizzards to *The Wonderful World of Disney*
Friends, while, in the background,
Two orange pills
Sing love songs
In tropical settings.

"What song is that they're singing?" Grubsy asks.
Mooshoo answers, "Not Chiquita Banana.
That's not for orange pills,
It's for yellow pills."
"This is getting too Cheechy, Mooshoo."
"I'd say, rather too Chongy, Grubsy."

"Opposition is true friendship," I breathe
Between gurgles of the bong.
"*Mannix!* Thanks be to God."
I pass the translucent plastic tube,
The color of a Mexican sunset, to Moo.
"The Exes we never feel
When sunset pies
Fall upon our eyes."
And then he drew a pillar of smoke
From the murky pond of goodness.

DESSERT Issue. June 1974.

The cover of the *Dessert Issue* recasts the boy
From the Concert for Bangladesh triple-album–
An emaciated eight-year-old boy
Seated behind a round, flat, shallow bowl
That could easily accommodate him
And twelve large potatoes–in dark chocolate.
His distended belly shines cocoa brown,
And a dainty bite, leaving traces of teeth,
Has been taken from his downcast head.
On seeing the cover, Grubsy
Tells his idea for a new
Fun kind of candy:
Shmiggles.
"Tiny chocolate-covered marshmallows
In shapes so inappropriate they make you giggle."
"Shame candy," adds Moo, "I like it."
Some suggestions generated include:

Grandma and Grandpa Walton
Fucking.
Archie Bunker and Meathead
Fucking.
Sanford and Son
Fucking.
Mary Tyler Moore and Bob Newhart
Fucking Ironside.
"Too Specific," Moo says.
"Those are for another candy:
Fuckles."
It's summer school now–
Make-up credits and on-campus employment.
The Student Union Store for Grubmonkey,
The Library for Mooshoo and me.
For all of us, tunes and pot and endless TV.
From our professor emeritus's chronic tube
We see Saigon's leftovers and Nixon's ruse.
And we love all the Patties in the news,
Making their counter-cultural debuts.
Patti, you know what your daddy said, Patti.
He said, "60 days ago she was such a lovely child.
Now here she is with a gun in her hand."
Hey girl, where you going with that gun in your hand?

As an offshoot of his newfound
Job-related interest in the inherent
Randomness of Library of Congress
Subject Headings
Mooshoo is collecting
The songs we listen to under some

New headings he hopes to introduce
To the library scientists.
He has invented:
Banal Assertions,
Banal Imperatives.

Under *Banal Assertions* he has, so far:
You Breathe The Air That I Breathe
You're Sixteen
You're Having My Baby
You Can't Always Get What You Want
You're So Vain
I Got Work To Do
I'm Takin' Care Of Business
I Shot The Sheriff
I'm A Ramblin' Man
I'm A Chiquita Banana
I Can't Get Enough Of Your Love
I'll Have To Say I Love You In A Song
I'd Like To Buy The World A Coke

Under *Banal Imperatives* he has, so far:
Let It Ride
Rock On
Get Down
Play That Funky Music
Let's Get It On
Touch Me In The Morning
Do It ('Till You're Satisfied)
Tie A Yellow Ribbon 'round The Old Oak Tree

At Work we can re-shelve

For hours and never stop
To acknowledge the jut
Of something foreign within us.
In our re-shelving haze
The library stays open forever,
Then burns to the ground
And now is a black square
For packing boxes filled
With munchies we may borrow
But not buy. How many Twinkies
Overdue, the wrappers left unread,
The fines compiling so I must
Work overtime in the stacks
Just to pay back the fines, regain
My privileges to borrow
Packages of Twinkies I can never
Actually open from the library
That stays open forever,
Burns down, and now is
A black square for packing boxes
Filled with munchies we may only
Borrow but never buy.
"Hell is other people's Twinkies,"
Observes Moo.
Grubmonkey is dismayed at my
"Most cruel and evil Twink-brary buzz,"
As he calls it. Gives me the remains
Of an O Henry bar he lifted from work.
"That one's already open," he says
With real empathy.

I've come home with
Poems and Essays
By John Crowe Ransom
And learn that, in addition
To watching TV,
With his poetry he aspired
To something marvelous
As green ice,
And with his criticism
Planted the seeds of
Kantian formalism in southern soil,
Cultivated his crop,
And watched it sprout into
A new kind of Wisteria-modernism.

In his observations about
The understanding of poetry, he explains
The idea of the concrete universal:
"That the Universal or logical
Plan of the poem is borne out
Perfectly in the sensuous detail
Which puts it into action;
And that this Concrete is used
Up so completely in the service
Of the Universal that there is no
Remainder."
No otiose surplussage.
No extra words.
None.
Not a one.

But this doesn't explain
What I'm watching now.
The mechanical magazine collage
Of *Monty Python's Flying Circus*
Acting out the Scopes Trial.
Professor Ransom
Conducting the puppets of
Bryan, Darrow and Judge Raulston
With the shame of an enlightened Tennessee
Poet whose first collection
Was titled *Poems About God.*
As the paper cutouts spin and swirl
Like rainbow lollipops
From Robinson's Drugstore,
J.C. addresses the jury of yokels,
"I anticipate the objection
That the name of God
Is frequently taken here
In ways that are not
The ways of the fathers,"
And then reads aloud
From Hunter's *Civic Biology,*
Text used by Scopes.
The chapter titled,
"Man's Place in Nature":
"In animal life,
From the Protozoa upward
There is constant change,
And the change is toward

Greater complexity of structure
And functions."

DEATH Issue. July 1974.

He has been still for days.
Grubmonkey is beginning to worry.
But somehow I know he's alive.
Technically, he is silent now.
But I can hear the lively salon *adieu*
His head is hosting.
It may be the latest batch of Kashmere
I'm presently inhaling,
Or the British Columbian *Champignons*
Grub shared with his best "shroomies"
Last night,
Or the echo of clown laughter
From the Bozo Nose acid tabs
I dropped last week.
Whatever it is, I have stepped
Through the looking glass
And find myself on a farewell safari *soirée*
In J. C. Ransom's noggin.
Marlin Perkins from
Mutual of Omaha's Wild Kingdom
Narrates.
There are no real swans,
only imaginary ones.
But the dream swans still suffer.
J.C.'s old friends The Fugitives,

Donnie Davidson, Al Tate, Bobby Penn Warren
Are all here to have a drink and say goodbye.
And hordes of wildebeest on the Serengeti Plain.
Someone uses a tortoise as an ashtray.
But you won't hear the tortoise
Complaining about ashes on his back
As he patiently advances
In the direction of a spilled martini.
The wildebeest—a large antelope—
grunts like a giant croaking frog.
People from the neighboring labs come.
Wake crashers. J.C. is an amiable host.
"Come in here. Come in.
You are not at a disadvantage.
Come in."
A small flock of ring-necked doves
Calling, just for
Some conversation,
Don't fly but modestly walk
Into the room.
Pretty soon they are all hiding
In the darkest, quietest corner.
Things are getting raucous.
Cheeky hyraxes and lizards play on the rocks.
A profusion of birds—
superb starlings, lilac-breasted rollers,
and polka-dotted barbets
fill the air with their songs.
"Bacchus, my friend," someone says.
"With friends like Bacchus,

Who needs purple anemones."
A tiny elephant jiggles a wine glass,
Gives the raspberry,
Passes out in a pompadour.
Robert Penn Warren
Leans over to Allen Tate:
"Al, there's something I must tell you.
The wildebeest would prefer
That you refer to them as gnu."
From an end table,
The little bush baby souvenir
With jiggling head becomes Nosferatu
Singing like Ethel Merman.
"The Forsaken Ethel Merman,"
Hyena Number One puns badly
On the title of a Matthew Arnold poem.
"You can't keep a good Merman down,"
Cackles Hyena Number Two.
"It tastes like chicken men of the sea,"
Adds Hyena Number Three, nibbling on a
Spitting-Cobra canapé.
As black-maned lions
Lounge in a tawny heap,
Hyena Number Four complains
Of Hyena Number Three,
"He's making a boudoir of himself.
He's making a bonbon out of everything.
He's making mockeries out of ribbon."
Leopards cough, cicadas tick.

A vulture alights on J.C.'s shoulder,
"Professor Ransom
I have a bone to pick with you."

But J.C. ignores the ugly bird,
And turns to a giraffe
Daintily nibbling leaves
From a thorny acacia tree.
"I aspired to
Green toothpicks.
They made my lips green.
Sometimes, late to the bar
My lips turned blue
In the bourbon."
The polite giraffe
Nods knowingly.

"Please, Professor Ransom."
It's my turn to ask a question.
"Kant's description of poetry
Is the description of a lyrical effect
Or of a moment of illumination.
And yet—what are we to say
About the long poems,
The philosophical ones,
The epic ones,
The goofy poetic dramas,
The crass poetic narratives?"

"Son, you see me sipping
From tiny sacks
Of *de rigueur* mortis,

Through the short straw."
His voice sounds so clear and right,
So *Roger,* as he speaks.

"Chances are, overwhelmingly,
That the Moral Universal
In such cases is a considerable
And organized sequence of ideas
Or events, embodied for action
And working themselves out;
Or, maybe they are
Ideas and events
Not clearly embodied,
But just talking themselves out;
And the best we can hope for
Is that there are some little poetries
Along the way, and perhaps a conclusion
Suited to the faith of a poet."
Laughter is over-heard behind the door
Of his unconscious,
And he is sure they're
Laughing about him.
"Don't worry son,
They're just animals
Of a different ilk.
We all have our distinct
Mating ways, our awe
And our love.
Mine was always
With those enchanted satires
For children,

So skeptical and magical at once.
That love will never die.
See, what is marked
Here on the remains
Of this tree, shattered
By the zebra stampede?
'Gulliver loves
Alice for ever and ever
In the Wonderland stables.'"

And then he slipped away.
With glittery sadness,
John Crowe Ransom
Died in his sleep, the third of July, 1974.
And left behind him
Some poems, some thoughts,
And a vast world, bewildered.

II. Office Machines

In Confidence

Acting out in secret,
Holding it in at the office,
Pretending I'm William Hazlitt,
Essayist of said orifice,
Receptionist with wit.

It's better than being jobless,
Considering I'm a postgraduate,
Making my name with promptness,
And getting things done lickety-split.
I am immediate.

I keep my workspace spotless,
All my pencils seriate,
My drawer is a necropolis,
For the surplus of retrofit,
As if I give a shit.

No one knows I'm a poet,
Holding it in at the office,
Inside weaving tercets,
But outside willing to submit
Their lists in triplicate.

Office Credo

Thy right hand, O LORD, is become glorious in power:
Thy ripe ham, O LARD, hath dashed in pizzas the anemone.
Exodus XV.6 (Translated from King James English
with dyslexia.)

This will be the office-
time of my existence

when little pictures of
venomous fish are cut out and

pasted up where they can't be
detected by executive staff.

Where peculiar memos are
passed on, filed, sometimes

lost in the shuffle and never
seen again, hopefully

recycled.
The very space of work

filled like cryptic
crosswords, with interruption,

cruel, passive-
aggression, bold submission,

with switchboard buzz,
then white-ed out

(*I'm* sorry)
by accident.

The desire to appeal to overseers.
The desire to appear

on assignment from above,
relentless typewriter tapping,

paper-crinkling
emerging, audible,

disclosing one little creed:
Noli me Tangere.

No Limit To my Anger
No Lime Tangerine

Target my Lonely Teenager
Eat my Meager Gnats Alone

Ogle the Meat Intern
Tint the Toilet Man Green

Learn to Tingle
The Genre Margin

Oil my Tangy Aroma
Moil me In Tangiers

Mohel me In Tangiers, Baby.
Moil me In Tangiers.

Special Cases (Previous Office Experience)

She, in the midst of all, preserved me still
A poet, made me seek beneath that name
My office upon earth, and nowhere else.
William Wordsworth

Mrs. Bortman, my supervisor
at the Jewish Family Services Office
believed in me, showed
me how to work the phones.

Within a week I knew
the locals of all my favorite
secret service officers,
I mean, social workers.

One sexy social worker
seemed so ditzy and sheltered
I was aroused thinking of her
in her office, in potential danger.

But most of the "clients"
(never call them "cases,"
Mrs. Bortman taught me)
were just lonely and depressed.

Like me! They posed no threat
but to themselves. Forsaken, and justifiably alone
some didn't care enough to bathe, while others
came dressed as if for a wedding.

One young Franco-New Brunswickian social worker sensed
my bittersweet personality and took me out for a beer.
He described in detail why he had been
circumcised at the age of thirty-five.

This was supposed to interest me
in his foreskin-less penis, but I just kept thinking
how painful it must have been for Abraham
to make his covenant so late in life.

The Wind Divider

Träumend an der Schreibmaschin'
saß die kleine Josephin'...
Gilbert and Profes

Hovered and swiveling behind the gray
cloth wall of her cubicle
divider, she has me seek into my drawer
for more than pencils. My rebel
typewriter girl who goes to the movies
alone soaring to screen
on the paper-clippèd wings
of my lighter/darker imagination.
Green ice-flashes of the Photostat machine
ignite her as St. Theresa in passion. She glides
past my station in white stockings
and Wallabees, red ones, like some devil nurse
prepared to I.V. the water cooler
with one scarlet ink cartridge.
Her hair black and shiny as trash bags
overstretched in their receptacles, so well groomed,
the best kept secretary, with airs, inviolable,
like a sadistic Veronica working in an office
just to spite Daddy. Or, my clean new American girl
as comfortable with Pitman as with Gregg,
tomboyish and undemanding, her fantasies
refillable, mine untold: (At the typewriter in a dream/
Sits my little Josephine... /My longing tapped
upon her keys/But she will need more keys than these...)
Spied through loose-leaf
reinforcements, I can smell fresh duotang,

taste the gluestick like sorrow on my lips,
hear the dust of rubber erasers
falling like little blackened frowns,
feel her like a pocket full of Parker Posey.

Notice to The Mayor (False Memo I)

Recently the pigeons of the city
have been marching along the river
with the tips of their outstretched
wings dabbed a conspicuous orange
color. This is contrary to the city's
policy of natural beautification.

I am writing as a concerned citizen
to you, he who is known for his capers
on the croquet field, for his shelves
of wives and mistresses, and his own
city of illegitimate children, all
of them bearing some form of his (your) name.

I suggest a plan of immediate action:
The pigeons shall be led (or forced,
as the case may be) into coops where
trained handlers will clip their wing-
tips, and then hold seminars on proper
urban conduct, stressing the prohibition
of orange in a poem about pigeons.

Translations (False Memo II)

A translation of Karl Kraus
reveals a luminosity of commas,

a pariah instinct, and the utter
un-translatability of the soul.

A small periodical bearing his name
is the sole resource of the era,

along with an eight hundred page drama,
consisting of everything, including

the punctuation of a brooding death sleep.
Some critics argue that very little or

perhaps nothing at all can be written
about a man's work. Others argue that

this is so only for those who did not
live in Vienna at the turn of the century.

Many Jewish scholars align him with the
most elemental moments of the Old Testament.

He is a vengeful god who desired the
absence of all but himself. Some call him

Germany's best kept secret, the source of a
literature that only those who have lived

in Germany can ever know. Once, Gertrude Stein
commented upon Kraus in a very long

sentence, with a single comma,
oddly placed. Karl Kraus hardly read English

and would have appreciated greatly,
Gertrude Stein.

The Office Boy

will do anything.

They have him moving furniture.

They have him erasing newspapers with liquid paper.

Once, when he was still an office baby,
he had a rattle
of thumbtacks
in a small
cardboard box.

Now he is a boy, and he will do anything they say.

They have him massaging the carpal tunnel out of
     The Assistant to the Executive Director's knotted talons.

And rubbing foot-oil on the Vice Chairman's cloven hooves.

They have him alphabetizing Kleenex tissues by the last
     names of their users.

Perforating smoked turkey slices into convenient, oblong tabs.

Funneling mayonnaise into empty glue syringes.

Re-bending paper clips into more "trendy and with it" shapes.

They have him raking muck from the women's urinals,

and lugging wet computers dry

in concentric circles.

He seems compliant now, but I fear

what he will do when he is an office man.

Lunch Receptionist Poems

Some things are set differently,
(i.e. the pencil sharpener has been moved)
making the composition of lunchtime poems
in the absence of lunch
most disheartening.

This book could be a list
of names:

SMITH, Karen
SOHA, Jim

and all the way down to

WHITSON, Wanda

That last name is no allusion to the postery
of inclusion, but is a real name.
Postery means poetry in typographical error.

There is a small yellow basket with some dry
earth in it, and it sits between two baskets.
Baskets was meant to read photographs,
but some people walked by and there was the anxiety
that this was not what I was supposed to be doing
(which is nothing) and so the lapse in concentration.

Looking for Geoff Bird:

Alisa Kablotsky wants to find him.
Any information will do.
She knows he's in New Jersey, but what town?
What is he doing there? Why is she looking
For him? What is she really looking for?

CROTCH, Cecil
LOVEROOT, Larissa
SILKTHREAD, Samantha
VINE, Vinny

Wanda has a great name
and so did Walt Whitman.

W.W.

Wanda Whitson with the collar of her shirt parted,
Addressing the pastoral envelope with corncob pen,
Licking the pre-industrial envelope with earthy tongue,
Eating lunch on the grass by the gothic brown cathedral,
Crumpling the remains in a brown paper bag discreetly,
Finding the pleats in her half-cotton dress sensuously,
Having risen in vertigo with nothing to grab onto,
Dazed during her walk, her return to the development office,
She once ran away with a corpulent programmer of computers,
She once had a child, but it died on delivery,
She moved from Seattle where the coastline is rugged,
She lived several years drugged on the mid-western highway,
She ambled her way like a bear to the east coast,
She found a freshwater pond, and she felt that it cleansed her,
She looked for a job in a real estate management office,
She looked for a job as a typist for a sports lawyer,
She took evening classes in French & Spanish history,
She looked for a job on the campus of The University,
The interview succeeded, the colander was porous,
The spaghetti was spun to mandolins a playin',
She started on Wednesday was welcomed aboard Thursday,
And some people liked her and some people didn't,
But she felt home enough to loosen her shirt collar.

Ivory Letter Opener (False Airmail Memo)

The egos on these bozos
won't fit into standard next-day
shipping boxes; are too heavy
to return to The Prick Zone.

Snug in its crocodile holster,
waits my cool ivory blade,
until our head Marketeer de Sade
shows a desire to re-upholster.

Then with my bone knife I'll be tusking
innocent and unsuspicious
envelopes and secret memos,
buckskin armchairs down to coil springs.

'Till then my words make me feel free,
and bluish bruises, red incisions,
are the checkered border of my signed
and sealed air-mail displacency.

To Upper Management with Gratitude Upon
My Recent Vivisection (False Memo III)

I accept your recent "Suggestions and Guidelines,"
sparked, I presume, by the growing height

of my Hall's Mentholyptus desk sculpture
(done exclusively on MY FREE TIME, actually,

not YOUR TIME, as you insinuate),
and my "Famous Missionaries as Cuddly Kitties"

screen savers. I had no idea that some of my Jewish
co-workers find my cuddlies "appalling" (as you put it).

I accept your "helpful tips" and "things worth thinking about"
with laughter, though they cut me open like a cat.

I don't care what anyone says, Sir Henry Morton Stanley
as a fuzzy York Chocolate youngun' IS adorable,

And the cherished David Livingstone
as a Ragamuffin-Cheetah lad is adorable AND

prophetic: His body is buried in Westminster
Abbey, his heart interred in Zanzibar.

But I suppose I must try not to expect so much
from people. Things like courtesy and understanding.

Why don't you just pinch my pineal gland
and draw the juice up like a tear through a straw?

Why don't you just eat my fish meat,
you motherfuckers, and choke on my bones

like ivory paperclips, like a spine of
alabaster staples. Choke on them, and die.

It's not the Tower of Babel, you freaks,
it's the *Taj Mahal*. The *Taj*.

Warwick Office Machines
(False Memo–Carbon Copy)

Attention all typewriters.
Across from Ann & Hope
there is a place for service
and supplies called Warwick
Office Machines. Call Jack
McKay if you have any complaints
about your machines, your office,
or about Warwick itself. Jack
is the kind of person who needs
other people to like him, so don't
let on that you're satisfied until
you are in possession of more
than you ever dreamed of having.
My present typewriter happens
to be baby blue in color, and
I LOVE IT. But you won't catch
me saying that to Jack.
Across from Ann & Hope.
On Old Post Road, in Warwick, R.I.
Your office machines will be forever
at your service.

Triumvirate Couplets (False Memo in Triplicate)

Triumvirates are really cool.
One to watch, two to duel.

One must brains, one must brawn,
One must facility with song.

Three must prevail, none must fall.
Triumvirates must three sets balls.

Triumvirates can omit words
And know that all is understood.

Troika. Trio. Triplicate.
Three times the anger to dilate

Thrice pair nostrils of trey noses.
And, post-ire pleasure in triple doses.

Triumvirate means three good guys.
Three hats, three belts, and misc. supplies.

Association based on pride,
Man-love, and a will to abide

By rule and law of all-for-one.
Triumvirate means three big guns.

Musketeers, amigos, men—
Triumviratees take vows, and then

Set out to prove themselves to each
Other, in firm triumvirate speech.

Announcements from the Offices of Hatman, Chalk & Fedora

Attention all typewriters.
There have been many titles
For this book, and for the men
Discussed in this book. But
The firm has decided
Upon the simplicity of its own
Name. The devotees of Hatman,
Chalk & Fedora will applaud
This decision despite aggressive
Proposals, minority reports,
Bitchy telexes, helpful suggestion cards,
Morbid memos–DANGEROUS
ADVICE–from outside parties.
The original title was, of course,
Important Men. An excellent title. But
Fedora (and Hatman, too, with his renowned
Treachery) insisted that only the most
Important of important men be named,
And that all others be executed.
Excluded, that is.
Please, Professor Ransom, or *Professor
Ransom, Sir!* or even more simply, *Professor
Ransom,* were proposed and enjoyed
And then rejected. *The Man Who Sells
Turnips* was proposed but not deemed
Worthy by Mr. Chalk, who is, despite the blue paper
Directives of his colleagues, the true Puppet
Master of this flat figure show.
Of the two titles proposed by

Some less politically seasoned members of
The Educational Puppetry Association,
The Puppet Book passed the
First round of the refereeing process
On the wings of its beautiful simplicity alone,
But was judged superfluous in
Round two, and *The Puppets and I*
Was never sent out for review, but was
Adored for its innocent stupidity.
THE TYPERINATOR, an anonymous
Suggestion, although admired,
Has been rejected in fear that
It originates in aphasia or
Typographical error, and not in genius.
Attention All Typewriters, the title,
Not the actual call for your attention, was
An exciting late suggestion, but was not
Submitted in time to meet the deadline
Set by Hatman & Fedora,
In the absence of Chalk
From the office.

#

Attention all typewriters.
The deadline has been extended.
Chalk is back in the office.
The title has been changed.
You must now forget all

Previous incarnations.
Get to work.

#

Attention all typewriters.
Paper must be handled
As though it is alive
With micro-tentacles.
Noise must be suffocated.
The urges of superiors must
Not be detained.
Dreams must not erupt
On the premises.

#

Attention all typewriters.
You must not talk
To yourself while typing.
This can cause
Illegitimate words
To appear on the pages
Of an adjacent typewriter
Without that typewriter's
Knowledge.
People can die
As a result.
It's not nice.
C'mon.
You know

Better than to talk
To yourself
In this place.

                #
Attention all typewriters.
Unconventional types
Must be imagined during
Your morning coffee break,
Or at lunch only.

                #
Attention all typewriters.
You know who you are.

III. Dark Drink

A Toast

To swimming bodies
that make an aqua-show
of death positions.

To souls in turquoise
puddles on white tiles.

To auburn beauty in a pool
with sprawling victims
of awkwardness.

To rusted eyes and eyes
compressed.

To burnt vagina
and corroded penis
soldered on wingless
angels.

To smeared halos, trailing
angel madness.

To drowned sex sinking
and memory struck numb.

Dark Drink

Let's see that bottle. Whew! That makes my eyes ache.
Ernest Hemingway

I dropped a bottle in the dark
and lost it there for many years

of daylight. From the dregs and up
through the hollow neck a spare man-

hood grew, straight and transparent,
like the sparse prose of a repressed war,

a straw from which to sip another self;
tight like the mouth of a narrow mouth jar.

Many years later, again in the dark,
I embraced the straw with my lips.

I took a deep drink of Ernest
Hemingway. How embarrassing

for a man, in this day and age.
The sun set, and there, in the dark

I found myself, one big Papa,
in full banana republic

regalia, drinking myself
into a stupor of sadness

without love or progeny, but
great sources of companionship

for speech and oblivion
at whatever dark watering hole.

•

We were all there together, each
his own significant virtue.

Mike was a bad drunk. Brett was a good drunk.
Bill was a good drunk. I was unpleasant

after I passed a certain point. Our words
were of drink in the dark. The dark

was where we found ourselves, repeatedly,
in others' throats. We reported

whether we remembered who we
were. Whether we were pleased or numb

with what we remembered or could
not remember. Or whether we cared, or not.

•

Sometimes Brett needed to destroy
herself before my eyes. I loved

her and was willing to oblige her.
We were neglectful of ourselves,

and frail. Cast off and set adrift
from the drunk continent. Immersed

in the cold, refreshing dark. I'd
stumble away from a *tête-*

à-tête with Brett, scattering loose
change like teeth on *taqueria*

floors. I wandered, the first sober
pilgrim at dawn, but drunk at night.

*CINZANO on the sidewalk
in dark letters.*

●

Slipping inside an establishment,
with all the consoling paraphernalia,

cold and translucent: glass, ice, liquor.
The clinks, and the barely-heard clinks,

chipped chimes resounding
in failing neon dimness.

These places, with heavy doors,
stools and glass swizzle sticks,

ascending bubbles, slices
of thick-skinned fruit all laid out,

are gleaming holes for us to crawl into.
Storage cells for our most

necessary amnesia, where you can swallow
Maraschino cherries until you are no longer.

When you are stained all red inside,
you can to speak to the olive-guy beside you.

●

Sometimes there was companionship,
the shared bewilderment of men

alone together. I enjoyed
the presence of men larger than myself

drinking their voices silent, lifting
glasses, tending their own dour faces with

awkward hands. We stared through each other for
hours and hours. It was good to be alone

in this company, and to depart
alone from this company.

•

Once, when I was the last man
sitting, *I drank a bottle of wine for company.*

It was pleasant to be drinking
slowly and to be tasting

the wine and to be drinking alone.
A bottle of wine was good company.

I sat across from the swinging
doors of the saloon.

The Bottle entered.
He was more like the rag inside

a bottle, the wet wick of a Roman
candle. He drank only wine, so I called

him Wine Bottle. *His white jacket*
was purple under the arms. The steam of

*wine hissed from his mouth. He must
drink a lot of wine,* I thought.

"Take me to your wine," he said.
I walked up the road and got out the two

bottles of wine. They were cold.
Wine Bottle followed me.

Some things—lost for so long in myself—
were surfacing, my shame-charm necklace

gathered thickly in my throat. *"You
have to drink plenty of wine to get it*

all down again," Wine Bottle observed. He
took one bottle and I took the other

bottle. *The wine was icy cold
and tasted faintly rusty. "That's not such*

filthy wine," Wine Bottle said. No, it was
not such filthy wine, and I could

breathe again. *Under the wine I
lost the disgusted feeling.*

•

I'm trying to remember
where I left my cigarettes:
The Salty Dog, The Cavern,
Moe's, Christopher's, Bernadette's,

The Mad Hatter, The Kilowatt,
The Elephant and Crown,
Le Saint-Sulpice, Baker Street,
Biddle's, The Saggy Sow,

La Cabane, Chicago's
Stanley Pub, The Peel Pub,
Les Bobards, Le Beaujolais,
The John Bull Pub, The Rub,

Café Sarajevo, Cheers!,
Sherlock's, The Albion,
Jello Bar, The Medley,
Jimbo's, Champs, Chameleon,

Les Beaux Esprits, Brutopia,
J.R.'s, Bistro Duluth,
Winnie's, Dalva's, Woody's, Shayne's
The Lime Light, L'Barouf,

VV (Vereingte Völker)
Taverna, Whiskey Café,
The Gold Spike, Old Pro,
Casanova's, Verres Stérilisés,

Sofa Bar, Le Swimming,
The Stork Club, Ramada Inn,
O'Greenberg's (Irish Yiddish
Coffee), Pip's, The Rusty Fin,

Thursday's, Bar Italia,
Silver City, The Typhoon,

La Maisonée, O'Looney's,
Clooney's, Reggie's, The Saloon,

Mad Dog in The Fog, La Cage,
The Limelight, Station 10,
Le Steppe, Club Soda, Kola Note,
Le Spectrum, The End.

•

For a while, instead of drinking,
I took to whittling the ends of anise

twigs and chewing them until
I had to spit. But then Brett found

me again, and requested me
for banality

before she ran with the true
banalistes later in the night.

We went out to the café to have an
apéritif and watch the evening crowd

on the Boulevard. They seemed so sober,
so lost in themselves, as Brett and I

prepared not to judge
each other. *"Well what will you drink?"*

"Pernod." "That's not good for little
girls." "Dites garçon, un pernod." "A pernod

for me too." It looked like hair-oil
and smelled like Italian Strega.

We let the drinks in.
A faint green light outlined the shape

of Brett's face. It was
how I looked as a boy.

•

Drunk and stupid at Pennyland
Arcades, we are a gang again.

A neat set. A clean body. Plugging coins
into the Voice-O-Matic, performing

our little skits of love. Mikey
taunts me with a microphone.

"Speak into the Mikey-phone!" Dr. Bill
develops his philosophy

of syrups and the sexes. Brett burlesques
her mother frying "whiskey tarts." "Frapracks!"

We play our bottles like glass flutes
and charm our snake. The snake bites himself and

dies. In unison, *"One hundred puddles
of spew in the stall…."* Bottles detonate.

Shiny brown shards of glass crunching
beneath us. Mikey doing his

old soft shoe, with calliope
and the bells of pinball. That lost

afternoon still somewhere on cardboard
Voice-O-Graph discs, our forgotten

coasters with the breath of alcoholics
preserved upon them.

●

Another night alone, I emptied one,
then another.

And then another. The contents
of each were lost forever. I ordered

more and emptied them in
turn. *The old woman looked in once*

and counted the empty bottles.
I was glad that someone was keeping track.

This way it would be known if I
ever went missing. I slipped an

empty one into my coat
pocket and moved onto the streets.

I leaned against a wall. I slipped
into an alley where the light

from the street could not find me.
I felt a shatter deep inside.

●

It all ended, one of my nights
of ellipses. The walls of The Stork Club

modestly dressed in gold tinsel
skirts. Each alcoholic his assignment

to keep him in the black, in the drink.
To keep the dark alive.

Dr. Bill retrieved bags of ice
from the freezer. Mike spun the mirror ball

to keep his glass full. Brett showed her
mole upon the bartender's request. *"You're*

drunk," some nosy motherfucker
said. *"Perhaps I am drunk,"* I replied with

a bottle in that cock-sucker,
punk-ass motherfucker's eye. Then barkeep

made me blotto, and I fell further down
the long, dark neck of the empty bottle...

beyond the realm of drink... further
into the dark... and I believe

I heard someone singing *"bury
the bottle with me...."* In the ground

and in the night, I dropped my bottle...
lost it there for many years.

From soil, from dregs and straight
up through the hollow neck, a spare

manhood... clean and transparent,
the sparse prose of a repressed war.

IV. Important Men

Important Men Refrains

THE HAT MAN delivers one with a bouquet
of roses and daisies and sweet yellow hay
to Mrs. Picaro, the hat man's most favorite lay
in the world.
Her head is too big for the hat.
Well, what do you think about that?
He'll have to refit her
and set a new time to come back.

*

O MR. MUSCLE MAN
walking along, kicking up sand.
He can crush diamonds
in his miraculous hands.
O Mr. Muscle Man,
can we feel your muscles?
All of the ladies are in a tousle
over your muscles.

*

THE MAN WHO SELLS TURNIPS
reclines in the alley,
he's sold enough turnips today.
The rest of his time
will be spent thinking,
thinking of new things to say—
About turnips, glorious turnips,
heavenly turnips, god-given turnips,
grown without sunshine, turned into moonshine,

curtseying turnips, tip-toeing turnips.
Reclined in an alley, his liver will burn up
one day.

*

Do you know THE MAN WHO WALKS ON ROOFTOPS?
He cries and cries, his tears cascade in drops.
Minuscule drops on the heads of the children.
Invisible drops on the heads of the children.
Tiny drops on the heads of the children.
Fatal drops on the heads of the children.
His crying never stops.
And he walks and walks and walks and walks
along the rooftops.

Water Dragon

Twelve years ago my love left me
for the war. He was no soldier
but he swore he must go
or else random accidents
would destroy our home.

"Take care of our little one,"
he said, pointing to this terrarium
and the strange sea creature that lived inside
on a tiny island, shielded only
by these thin glass walls.

Light from one flickering, yellow bulb
was all the food the water dragon
needed to survive. Likewise, my hope
and comfort fed on the flickering
of some remote war.

I used to watch the dragon
pace the strand,
survey the water
that I changed religiously,
afraid that parasites were there.

Once I even touched its skin
and let its threadlike tongue
draw gleams of tea
from a spoon
my lover left with me.

I clutched my arms
in my sleeping gown
and watched the monster breathe

beneath the little mango tree–
fallen now, and petrified.

What can it mean?
I fear what it can mean.

Last night before I went to sleep
I thought I heard a whispering
and rose to find the amber bulb
had left a million glistening shards
across the dragon, lying dead.

The Energy King

These are horrible, streaking lines.
It's all so embarrassing, the zipping

and zapping sounds from erogenous zones,
the chaotic grid, translucent and alive

between my elbows and my hips, ignored
politely by Ramrodrigo, my last

faithful slave found on these palace
floors, marble, thankfully a poor conductor.

Sirrah, fetch me a pith-ball. Bring
me the cat fur from the Queen's bed chamber,

and some children to entertain—
the ones she never bore me, barren child,

but alas, even she no longer haunts
my palace memory, gone in a crisp—

and teach the laws that pour forth from my royal fold.
Such frail lightning, such uncommon streaks

of fire. Go build me a pyre;
no precious metals, but the finest woods

from my abandoned forests, coined and wrought
into abundant metal-looking things.

Then sacrifice an animal for me,
a pigeon, or a swan,

once a month, no matter what the skies warn,
or what they do. And then tell the story

of your eclectic master's jealousy
against everything winged and translucent,

against the very gods he did not think
existed, or were godlike, if they did.

Good Rammy, I hover now,
but soon this energy will lose

its shape (however nebulous)
completely, and only you will know

the glow, this transparency of arrogance,
the source of all my woe, and my Queen's

death. When she suggested I looked silly–
while truly, all afloat and alight, I resembled

a luminous bird of human form–
I became (no doubt, overly) incensed.

So, in your prayer upon my pile
you may omit the dead,

the reason for the fire (my swollen pride),
the pitiless destruction of my bride,

and concentrate instead upon the light–
the texture of white flashes, green flashes–

and when you decide upon a refrain,
let it have the instant I disappeared.

Mr. Chalk

I have visited the offices of Mr. Chalk.

It was just as you said it would be,

With the shelf of peculiar microphones along the back wall.

He explained how each microphone owns many voices.

When he dozed in the armchair he seemed to wheeze with
   subtle emphasis.

Through the noise I thought I heard a radio play,
   "Enlightenment for Children."

He is a serious man, your Mr. Chalk.

How did you meet him?

I know you told me, but I can't remember.

Here's a curious thing, perhaps.

As I entered he said to me, "When it is gone you must bring
   it back."

I thought the "it" must refer to you.

To avoid responding, I put my hand into an urn filled with
   buttons.

He insisted I take as many as I desire.

But I am uncertain how many buttons I desire.

He hasn't a clue about us, does he?

I only ask because he kissed my ear with pursed lips.

And I suspect he speaks to me while I sleep.

I feel his voice somewhere in my spine.

Last night I dreamed I tried to kiss you.

My mouth was a false pocket, buttoned shut.

Mr. Fedora

The bridge is blocked and there's a blacksmith's din,
There's no getting off this island unless you can swim,
And the local kids' T-shirts say "I was born in sin."
There's no architecture to admire, no flora:
So I step into a bar called Mr. Fedora.

Eight men in derbies, four punks in berets,
Two anemic girls bearing plywood trays,
"All strangers shall die," I hear one of them say,
"We are the survivors of Sodom and Gomorrah.
"We are the morbid children of Mr. Fedora,
The morbid children of Mr. Fedora."

Well, I order a drink and bite into an egg.
I hear one of the derbies, the one missing a leg
say, "When you drink here you better drink to the dregs.
"It's what remains of those who've come before ya,
"And such is the law of Mr. Fedora.
"Such is the rule of Mr. Fedora."

On the wall there's a fish with a crimson tail,
And a narwhal tusk from one of those corpselike whales,
With scarlet stains from the lives it's impaled.
And from the back room comes a fiery aura.
We all sense the presence of Mr. Fedora.
We sense the approach of Mr. Fedora.

His face is all hat with an evil eye.
His impeccable shoes have a hellish shine.
His voice is not of the human kind.
He says, "Now that you've come,
I hope you're prepared to die."

And the games continue, the poker and the pool,
The tricks with the knives and the assassins' duels,
The desecration of the legitimately cruel,
And the sex and injections and more, yeah.
All for the pleasure of Mr. Fedora.

I'm searching my memory for answers and quotes.
For the ingredients of ancient antidotes,
As their previous violences burn in my throat,
I appeal to the Koran and to the Torah,
To help me break the rule of Mr. Fedora,
To help me soil the shoes of Mr. Fedora.

Now, one of the punks is holding one of the girls,
And with a billowing blade he cuts into her curls,
And he's ready for her to depart from this world.
"Have mercy," I say, "I implore ya!"
But he waits for a sign from Mr. Fedora.
He waits for a word from Mr. Fedora.

The Fedora turns to me and prepares his threat.
He says, "You have come here as an immigrant.
"And now you dare to speak of our need to repent?
"Let's get it on now, I'll take you to the floor, yeah.
"'Cause I'm your living hell, I am Mr. Fedora,
"And I love to kill, I am Mr. Fedora."

Well this was the time for the angels to come,
To take hold of my arms and to turn and run,
To carry me off on a course to the sun,
To feel the consoling strength of The Holy One.

But they weren't around, the angels were a no-show,
There was no safe place for me to go,
So I just stood my ground and moved painfully slow,
And prepared for a banquet of gore.
The meat would either be me, or Mr. Fedora.
It was gonna be me, or it was gonna be Mr. Fedora.

He came at me with a hideous lust.
So, I made my move for the narwhal tusk.
I held it firm, and I took my thrust.
I punctured that bastard to the core.
I made a lollipop with a tilted fedora,
I made a bloody sucker of Mr. Fedora.

I propped him up like a dead drunk at the bar,
Took a final taste of my drink from before,
And my look told the others I was ready for more.
But they just stood there like the orphans of a war.
So I claimed my new hat, and I stepped through the door.
I felt good in that hat as I stepped through the door.

Language Monster

I'm so afraid of the Language Monster.
He's fallen sly and dumb.

In his sleep his letters prosper.
Soon a simple sound may stun.

If he tells me that I've lost her
I must find my secret gun

and make excuses as I foster
other lies to lead him on

into the chamber where he tossed her.
With the wheel she spun

I'll capture me the Language Monster.
I'll ring his letters' necks for fun.

I'll spread his body out across the
spokes in view of everyone.

I'll dispossess the Language Monster
of his fertile tongue,

until an utter silence prospers
and all speaking is undone.

Important Message

When your red lights glow,
and your broad throat groans,
I know your hunger is stirred
for a platter of stones.

You can swallow them softly,
feel them travel your body,
and when your stomach is full
your tongue can move hotly.

I never learned how to fight,
but I'm very polite.
And my impotent screams
leave dull streaks of light,

like a neon marquee
against clouds moving darkly,
in my mercurial head.
I hope you can hear me.

Unknown Leonard Cohen

These foreign voices hold my foreign tongue.
And my black suit has nothing in it save
The well abuséd corpse of a blank knave,
The better on a hanger to be hung.

Unless a tree be made available
For artifice on nature there to swing,
And from its closing throat to softly sing
Whatever darkness that seems saleable.

This is a love song, and I'm good at it
Because I still have you to torture me.
I dreamed I saw your body on TV,
But it did not arouse me, not a bit.

And even if I held you now in claws,
My success in hunting is my loss.

I am the unknown Leonard Cohen,
Parallel legend, parody's clone.
Just back from heaven, on my way home,
Traveling alone.

With every constant person that you know,
There is a ruthless tailor with his knife,
There is a secret partner in his life,
There is a worshipper of sorrow.

There was a row of houses on the street,
Each an alternative for my life.
But none would take my children or my wife,
So I left them all and walked down to the beach.

The strand was very bright with a huge sky,
And miles of sand, I knelt and said a prayer
To the falling bombs. I didn't care
That every single door was a closed lie.

In every falling object that I see,
There is an angel trying to get free.

Magnetism

Short of declaring then and there that he loved her,
there was absolutely nothing more to say.
F. Scott Fitzgerald

Canisters of pictures behind
radiant eyes of our magnetic hero,
Mr. George Hannaford,
a star of the silver screen,
and lover in between,
of anyone who has ever seen
the straight of his back,
the curve of his lips controlling words
that are so moving one would call them obscene
if one did not know sterling George.

From the age of twelve Kay Tompkins had worn
her men like rings on her defenseless fingers.
Playing small parts in the exciting Ziegfeld shows,
she met George, already a star
of the recent "natural" type
just then in vogue.
In him she found a sense of hope.
And with her confident eyes
she secured her prize,
and hardly thought before she spoke.

(Say whatever comes to mind.)

In every true Hollywood romance
there must be a love triangle, or rectangle.
I'll implicate myself and one more,
let's call her Elizabeth
my Queen of Beauty.

So, Kay and George and me and my Queen
all went on a trip, say, barracuda fishing.
And just as soon as Kay had me hooked by the heart,
George had Eliza wishing
that she could have a moment alone to touch his eyes
and see what else might come of that,
while I tried to devise some subtle way
to stroke the hair inside Kay's hat.

(Say whatever seems to charm
without doing harm.)

And afterwards with drinks at the bar
we spilled our desires onto our chosen strangers' laps.
And then we lived out our dreams,
we had our flings,
our jealousies, our savage fights, our painful anger,
and other things.

In every true Hollywood romance
there must be a love that is assured to last.
The last time I saw our Mr. George Hannaford,
he stood alone, he stood so tall, he stood so cold
with a Martini glass.

Important Men Action Figures

... the Author diminishing like a figurine at the far end
of the literary stage...
Roland Barthes

"Salty" the Sailor Lost at Sea
"Weepy" the Jailor in the Penitentiary

Handkerchief Hobo Asleep on Boxcars
Mucousy Joe Smoking at the Cash Bar

Bone China Waiter Crushing Crab Shell
"Tea-Bag-Eyes" the Day-Trader Waiting to Sell

Breath-Mint Banker Securing a Lock
"Old Locky-Knees" the Spelunker Stuck in a Rock

Peanut Shell Sports Fan Spilling his Beer
Stuffed Dalmatian-Hide Fireman Hanging on at the Rear

Graphite Composite Tennis Pro Hitting a Volley
Minced Meat and Ketchup "Sloppy Joe" Eating Cannoli

"Li'l Carrot Top" the Left-Winger in a Trench Coat
Cherry Jell-O Nightclub Singer Holding a Note

Voice

Told to find my voice
I popped out my eyes
And swallowed them.

My eyes saw nothing
So I sliced off my ears
And swallowed them.

My ears heard no voice
So I swallowed tongue,
Hands, nose, etc.

Still no voice of mine
Was found, just a rood
Speaking in someone else's dream.

Vibriosis

Written with, for, and somewhat about Todd Swift

A shiny Mercedes, a bald ape
named Gabor,
both purring like pink leopards
on a mercury chain.

Ron the American
owns The Coliseum Club,
wants to do business
in his office, hands me over

to the crackling voice
on the other end,
a friend of the Minister
of Permission.

The salamander
with the monograph collar–
"Walter"–
straddles the lean arm of Fruszina.

We are all in harmony
with the alligator interior,
hurtling like heads
between Gladiators.

Ron arranges a line of coke
on each of her thighs
and like a brutish mole
burrows down the middle.

Fruszina gasps it up,
an expert in dying,
she has been caught by the legs,
her fox fur beading blood.

Civilization is scratched
and keeps crooning, "… there we are…
there we are… there we are…"
in vibratile discontent.

All they want is my genius.
I give them names: Hatman,
Chalk, and the quisling snitch-fink,
Fedora.

A shame to be a coward,
but then, who wants liver,
when there's leopard
to eat?

In the Coliseum grotto now,
Mr. Nagy–The Permissioner–
fillets a ferret
with a feral grin,

a Polish assassin's intestines
thrown–a casual sash–
across his shoulders:
"She was a deadly whore," he mutters

sadly. Fruszina consoles him,
stroking his vibrissae

and murmuring dictaphonia
from her smashed voice box.

Mute Gabor mimics
her love upon a blue peacock
with the four-fingered hand
he favors.

Sometimes, in hell, Ron
is uncertain of his identity,
so infernally close to loss
that he hardly recognizes himself.

I know it's all over, for them too.
I see the S-shaped disease,
its trembling migration
toward our deepest stations.

Fruszina cuts herself on a whisker.
Two Russians with style enter
bearing bowls of warm cholera
to anoint me with, slowly.

Stick Men

Without faces,
their curved backs
betray a longing for substance.

Their dainty stick feet
float as random
marks on a page.

The sad spines of parents
holding the tiny stick hands
of their tiny stick children,

sterile uncles and cousins
bearing grievous loads
where threadlike arms meet spindly breasts.

Stick Man Complaining

We have had to walk forever
on this spotless plane, monotonous.

My wife is dead, and I don't cherish
her memory. She left years ago,

fallen like an arrow, pointing
the endless line before me

and my son, who hasn't grown
these many years. He steps with me

and never lifts his stunted head
to see if we have arrived.

He was born here on the walk,
and he's better made for it

than I am. We have no need to stop,
no needs at all, being stick men:

moving wicks that, legend says,
are meant to bear the glowing joy

and anguish of fuller beings.
What was it then that made her stop?

I don't mourn her absence
but wonder at it, the only space

of its kind in this steady stream
of hobbling sticks. "Mercy,"

she said, but my shrinking boy,
thankfully, cannot hear:

ears were never meant to grace
the lobe atop his neck.

What good can come from standing still?
From planting the body like a rod?

From falling forward to the ground,
dissolving into the clean plain?

I looked back for as long as I could,
but I have never understood.

I'm not equipped to care
about a pageant of despair.

V. Quaker Oats

Daddy Lazarus

It occurs to me that I am America.
I am talking to myself again.
Allen Ginsberg

America is so confessional. Wide mouth plastic bottles of
   Coke, Pepsi, Dr. Pepper, 7-Eleven Big Gulps of Mountain
   Dew, Jumbo Slurpees and melted Rocket Pops spilling
   Old Glory puddles of blue and red.
Canada is a carton of milk left outside in winter, expanding
   when frozen. The carton wobbles like a pointed silo on
   the kitchen table.
Europe is a continent of little porcelain houses filled with
   liqueur, chimneys stoppered with bitter wax to keep both
   Americans and Canadians from drinking them empty.
I don't know Africa. I don't know The East. I must confess.
This will be more American, than anything.
I cannot tell a lie.
It all started when I moved to Boston in the year of the
   First Gulf War.
The first words scribbled in my Boston University National
   Brand Easyperf 100 Sheet College Ruled notebook are
   "Quaker Oats." Oats is underlined. It seems oats were
   important, but I can't remember why.
Other entries in these early pages of my notebook include
   R. K. Martin's *The Homosexual Tradition in American Poetry,*
   Wentworth and Flexnor's *The Dictionary of American Slang,*
   The Quakers by A. Barbour, *Delmore Schwartz's America*
   by Irving Saposnik, and Ariel J. Hansen's *Expatriate Paris:
   A Cultural and Literary Guide to Paris of the 1920s.*
I was writing my own *Baedeker* to expatriate Boston in
   the early 1990s.

I was one expatriate. My roommate David (a friend from
  High School) was another. My other roommate, Peter,
  a fellow literature student, was from Chicago, but had
  been to Paris. Good enough. *Cheers* was the #1 show
  in America.

David worked on *The New England Quarterly* and had a
  photographic memory. He remembered everything he
  saw on TV.

In high school he was the only one who scored perfectly
  on my friend Adam's "Officially-Humiliating-Utterly-
  Impossible-Except-for-Me-The-Author-*M*A*S*H*-Quiz."
  (100-plus questions.)

David remembered that Charles Emerson Winchester III
  graduated Harvard Medical School in 1943, that Colonel
  Potter's granddaughter's middle name was Pershing, that
  Radar's hamster's name was Dopey, and that his tortoise
  had no name at all (a trick question).

David had a cat named Nixon (the truth) who sat on top
  of the television and sometimes got his paw in Colin
  Powell's face.

We saw no Frank or Charles between us. We believed
  ourselves all Hawkeyes and Trappers and (to a lesser extent)
  Hunnicuts.

So there I am.

I am sitting on my futon, surrounded by dark wood-panel
  walls in an Allston, Massachusetts apartment, reading
  the *Diary of Laura Palmer,* the intimate confessions of
  a television character.

One of the diary entries runs as follows: *And then he said,
  "Is that a growth? Is that a large growth or a fuzzy baby limb?"*

I was so embarrassed. Mortified. Until he touched it, and looked at me and said, "Whatever it is, I think it's really cute." He is sooo *sweet.*

Another diary entry runs, *All those words that do not appear in this sentence because these words appear instead. And in this sentence. And in this one.*

Another one runs, *I am channeling the lost lyric poetry of Franz Kafka, and soon it will all be found in the pages of this diary. In these poems, the animals are real animals. They do not stand for anything. They are intolerant and lazy, lounging like blue tigers in the shade.*

During that first week I also read Kafka's *Amerika,* and it helped me get my bearings.

Autumn semester, I order provolone and Genoa salami at Boston Market Deli. I puke outside Harper's Ferry Bar & Grill, and am compliant at the site of the old South Boston Aquarium.

I study Proust and often find "that delicious vagueness, rich in expected surprises, which is romance."

For instance, I am taken on guilt trips through the offices of the *Partisan Review* by an adorable (despite her psoriasis) Pawtucket Melvillian. I eat the home cooking of a blond Biloxian Faulknerian. I share intimate childhood secrets with a 6' 2" Toledo Dreiserian.

Meanwhile, Peter cannot commit to his own beautiful Princess who has followed him to Boston from Albuquerque, because he is newly in love with a Parisian exchange student.

America is a fine place to sow one's wild (sugar frosted) oats.

But, by November, Peter lay upon a bed of leaves ready to act
the death scene in his own broken play, and I found my
objects of desire too intellectual, too neurotic, too sickly–
too like myself for me to really love them.

Peter was leaving personal notes for David in our Fridge.
Things like: *Keep your fucking paws off my Orange Juice or
I'LL KILL YOU.*

David would reply with little notes of his own, like: *I may
have spit on your leftover Lasagna, but I can't say for sure.*

I could not resist contributing to the epistolary novel that
was materializing in our ice box with notes like: *My Cream
Cheese has developed insomnia and a nervous stutter because
of the tension in here.*

Two anonymous replies:

Your Cream Cheese can eat me.

Your Cream Cheese can bend over and spread 'em.

In short, facts were not merely finding a footing-place in our
history but they were usurping the domain of Fancy and
invading the kingdom of Romance.

That was Oscar Wilde on the decay of lying.

The decay of lying was caused by America. America is a fine
place to lay oneself bare. To tell it like it is.

January 15th, 1991. *The war begins?* (My notebook reads.)

I write carelessly so that nothing that is not green will survive.

William Carlos Williams wrote that.

Aaron, one of my teachers that year, told us about a poetry
reading he went to in which a feminist poet kept repeating
"Williams Carlos Williams" in one of her poems, the "s"
added to the first William to signify the poet/doctor's

chiasmatic patriarchal oppressiveness. At first Aaron was
   just annoyed, but then he saw the humor in it.
Williams Carlos *Williams*. *Williams* Carlos *Williams*.
   Williams Carlos *Williams*.
But at this point in history–January 15th, 1991–I'm not yet
   American enough to do something like that in a poem.
I'm still just barely daring to breathe or Achoo.
I'm still just barely discovering you.
O America, I'm just beginning to see and smell and taste you,
in the beautiful water off Nauset,
in the leathery pocket of my baseball mitt,
or in the last of my Canadian Raisin Glossettes.
Lounging in front of the TV,
just David, Peter, Nixon and me.
This is what we see:
Patriot Missiles Taking Out Scuds
12 Patriots Fired Makes 12 Scuds Duds
33 Launched 33 Destroyed
42 Hits For 42 Deployed
48 Fired 48 Threats Erased
Keeping Us Safe In The United States.
If the path of one missile
crosses the path of another missile
it is officially recorded as a direct hit.
It's like throwing letters
(intimate, confessional letters)
at a zip code.
0   2   1   3   4
Send it to ZOOM!
To find America, try this recipe at home:

To find America, I crossed out every sentence that doesn't
  mention drinking in Ernest Hemingway's *The Sun Also
  Rises*. Then I copied the lines that remained into my
  Boston University notebook. Seven notebook pages of
  sentences highlighting all that intimated impotence.
  On the Fourth of July, on our Allston porch, I read these
  sentences aloud to Peter and David. And then we went
  out to the café to have an aperitif and watch the evening
  crowd on the Boulevard.

And a million more people glide by.
Two teenagers are getting high.
Nothing yet has appeared in the sky
on this Fourth of July.

That's from a song I wrote at the time.

Actually, there are no Parisian Boulevards in Boston, but
  Comm. Ave. split in half by The T. No aperitifs, but paper
  cups of tartar sauce and creamy clam chowder. No cafés,
  but plenty of O'Brien's O'Leary's O'Malley's to hide inside.
  Instead of "in public" we expatriates in New England
  commune in Puritan privacy on the verdurous porches
  of clapboard houses, or on couches in dark family dens.

On our Sally Ann sofas we are as American as Walt Whitman
  leaning and loafing on the grass. Still, we went out to
  celebrate American Independence on the banks of the
  Charles.

We got high and watched yellow ribbons flutter in the trees.

Next day I went to work at the Boston University Alumni
  Office as a part-time receptionist and general office
  assistant.

On one of my lunch hour shifts at the reception desk I won a
    BU commemorative wristwatch by submitting fifty slogans
    for the coming year's fundraising campaign, including
    what I thought was a sure winner:
Make Us Rich Like Boston Cream Pie University.
But they went with the professional PR team's slogan, *BU,*
    Be Proud, Be Generous.
BS, Be Parodic, Be Genoese (like Christopher Columbus).
I composed this–slogan number fifty-one–while setting the
    time on my new Boston University watch.
On other lunchtime occasions I typed my lunch-receptionist
    poems *à la* Frank O'Hara *à la* Nicholson Baker *à la*
    Wallace Stevens *à la* Dilbert.
À la peanut butter sandwiches.
That was The Amazing Mumford, I think.
So you see, I *have* been to America. I have written my
    American poem.
I know how it feels to be in America during wartime.
I know how to find myself. How to find myself in America.
I can tell you how to get, how to get to Sesame Street.
It's in Philly, I think, not Boston.

Yom Kippur (California, 1998)

Suit-less and unwashed for over a month.
A half-ass, last minute dart into the university
hall for a makeshift reform ceremony on folding chairs.
I never thought I'd miss reading in unison,
or responsively, so much.

So much for adding a new wool blazer
to my closet for this traditional occasion.
So much for the uncomfortable shirts my father
buys me to euphemize the stretched-cotton szchlob
who begins seven new notebooks a week.

A weak family memory in the body of a thirty-one-
year-old younger son, but with a strong sense of having
come specifically from somewhere. And this family fear
        of weakness?
My smartest (weakest) friend has noticed it in me
and asked, "What's wrong with being weak?" Nothing.

Nothing, but don't touch me. Nothing, but I don't want
to be among those who have failed to survive.
I don't think you would have made it,
but I will remember you to my children.
They will find you always in my eyes.

My eyes scan the auditorium for a pretty
young Jewess to marry. Someone I can bring home,
but also to an exciting climax. Three prospects,
pretty young girls sitting alone. But
I leave before Kol Nidre, too weak to hold fast,

too hungry inside to wait for the sun to go down.

Frontier Thesis

The Crocodile Cowboy
plays with his hope toy.
It's something to enjoy.

Bent out of fortune,
he's not the only one
to swallow a whole gun
in the name of fun.

These words have nothing,
but new ones are coming,
and if I know one thing
it's that the currents are running

from his eyes through the sky.
If you have opinions,
well, that's none of my business.

You see, the frontier's been captured
and turned into disposable matches.
The white line is fractured
memoriam patchwork.

A bourbon head radio
spins out a "yo yo."
When the ghost voice yells go go
it's really breathing with sorrow.

The dead reeds are whistling
a poem of distance.
The white locust jawbone

taps out a bone song
for the Crocodile Cowboy,
all the way home.

Charlotte Gainsbourg

I saw Charlotte Gainsbourg
in California
leaning against a car.
She seemed kind.
Charlotte Gainsbourg
in California.
I admired her eyes
and her face from a distance.
I would have said hi,
but I was too shy.
And I think I could die tonight.

For Charlotte Gainsbourg
near San Francisco.
I wonder where she'll go
after the show?
I don't know this city,
but it is lovely
seen from a distance,
seen from above.

And her father could write a song.
Her father sang badly, but he was stronger
than I'll ever be
while I'm in this country.
I am not from here,
and neither is she.
I mean Charlotte Gainsbourg
looking so lonely

in California.
Please take me away.
I feel I could die tonight.
And I'm hooked on nicotine.
And I'm hooked on actresses in their teens.

I have to read
a book by Nathaniel
Hawthorne the nineteenth-
century writer.

I have to read
a book by Nathaniel
Hawthorne, a romance
written while he
was away from America.

I saw Charlotte Gainsbourg
in California,
leaning against a car.

Notes

The speaker in "Bewildered" cannot possibly be me, since I was only seven years old in 1974, and thus could not have been an undergraduate at Kenyon College in the year John Crowe Ransom died. (Similarly, many of the other seemingly autobiographical poems in this book are actually written in character.) The poem was inspired by an anecdote Robert Allen told me about the time he lived next door to Ransom in 1974. Allen, who could see into Ransom's living room from his adjacent cottage, noted that the elderly poet and teacher watched television to the exclusion of pretty much everything else. The particular issues of *National Lampoon* mentioned in the poem do in fact exist. The Scopes or "monkey" trial, concerned with the teaching of evolutionary theory by substitute biology teacher John Scopes, took place in Dayton, Tennessee in 1925, with Clarence Darrow as leader of defense, and William Jennings Bryan, leader of the prosecution. The zoologist, Marlin Perkins hosted the popular wildlife television show *Wild Kingdom* in the 1960s and 70s. William Hazlitt (mentioned in "In Confidence") was a late romantic man of letters who penned such essays as, "On Depth and Superficiality," "On the Pleasure of Hating," and "On the Qualifications Necessary to Success in Life" (these three titles all published in 1826). The epigraph to "Special Cases" comes from William Wordsworth's *Prelude* (1805 version, Book X, ll. 918-920), and refers to his discovery of the vocation of poet after some unsettling time he spent in France. The Gilbert and Profes lyrics that appear as an epigraph for "The Wind Divider" are my translation of the German text cited in Friedrich Kittler's *Discourse Networks 1800/1900* (Stanford, 1990. p. 358). Karl Kraus (1874-1936)—mentioned in "Translations"—was a satirical essayist, playwright, poet and aphorist who did most of his writing in Vienna. Walter Benjamin quotes Brecht as having said about Kraus: "When the age laid hands upon itself, he was the hands." (Walter Benjamin, "Karl Kraus," *Reflections*. Trans. Edmund Jephcott [Schocken Books, 1983. p. 253]). Some of the names in "Lunch Receptionist Poems" are taken from words that appear in Walt Whitman's "Song of Myself." The story of David Livingstone (1813-1873) the missionary, and Sir Henry Morton Stanley (1841-1904) the journalist/adventurer–two heroic figures adored by the speaker in "To Upper Management With Gratitude"–is told by Stanley himself in his published diary, *How I Found Livingstone: Travels, Adventures, and Discoveries in Central Africa, Including an Account of Four Months' Residence with Dr. Livingstone* (1874). Stanley's diary is the source of the famous greeting, "Dr. Livingstone, I presume!" Some of the potential titles alluded to in "Announcements from the Offices of Hatman, Chalk & Fedora" were suggested by Todd Swift and Jon Fiorentino. *The Puppet Book* (1965) and *The Puppets and I* (1950) are actual books on educational puppetry published by Faber & Faber. The epigraph, and all the italicized portions of "Dark Drink" are actual lines pertaining to alcoholic beverages that appear in Ernest Hemingway's *The Sun Also Rises*. "Water Dragon" was inspired by Andrew Marvell's "The Nymph Complaining for the Death of Her Fawn" (1681), and televised reports of the Second Gulf War. The idea for a radio play entitled, *Enlightenment for Children* (mentioned in the poem "Mr. Chalk") comes from an actual series of radio shows aimed at educating children about historical, natural catastrophes that Walter Benjamin delivered from 1929-1932. These radio shows *(Aufklarung für Kinder)* are discussed in Jeffrey Mehlman's book, *Walter Benjamin for Children, An Essay on His Radio Years*

(University of Chicago Press, 1993). The line "eight men in derbies, four punks in berets" in "Mr. Fedora" was inspired by the poem "xiii 5" from e. e. cummings's 1925 collection *XLI Poems.* Some of the characters in the poem "Magnetism" come from an F. Scott Fitzgerald short story that was first published in *The Saturday Evening Post* (3 March 1928) under the same title. The epigraph to "Important Men Action Figures" comes from Roland Barthes's essay, "The Death of the Author," available in most literary theory anthologies. As far as I know, all of the types listed in that poem are imaginary, and are not available at a store near you. Bestselling items from my imaginary line of *Important Men Personal Hygiene Products,* include: Hugo Boss Dental Floss, John Stuart Mill's Weight Loss Pills, The Lord Byron Curling Iron, and, locally, the irresistible Leonard Cohen Testosterone Cologne. "Vibriosis" was written in email exchange with Todd Swift. Swift published his own version of the poem, entitled "Greatness Flicker," in his e-book *Elegy for Anthony Perkins* (Rattapallax Press, 2001, pp. 16-17). The title of the poem, "Daddy Lazarus," was created, of course, by grafting the titles of two Sylvia Plath poems. The epigraph to "Daddy Lazarus" comes from Allen Ginsberg's "America." I have in mind, in particular, the sound recording of Ginsberg's recitation of that poem at Town Hall Theatre in Berkeley, 1956 (available on the CD, *Holy Soul Jelly Roll: Poems & Songs [Rhino Records, 1994]*). There are many references to other American poems in "Daddy Lazarus" that I will not list here. Frederick Jackson Turner first articulated his "Frontier Thesis" in the essay, "The Significance of the Frontier in American History," which he read at the American Historical Association's annual conference of 1893. Actress "Charlotte Gainsbourg," daughter of Serge

Gainsbourg and Jane Birkin, was in attendance at the 1992 Mill Valley, CA film festival where *The Cement Garden,* directed by her uncle Lawrence Birkin, was presented.

Acknowledgments

Some poems in this collection have previously appeared (sometimes in different versions) in the following journals and anthologies: *New American Writing, Parchment: Contemporary Canadian Jewish Writing, Career Suicide* (Montreal: DC Books), *Matrix Magazine, 100 Poets Against the War* (Cambridge: Salt Publishing), *Queen Street Quarterly, Rampike, Short Fuse* (New York: Rattapallax Press), *Journal of Literature & Aesthetics,* and *Slingshot.*

Thanks to J. W. Stewart for the Galton/Magritte Typewriter Man, and the imaginary, (hand-drawn!) typewriter keys on the cover. Thanks to Dave, Terry and Heather Pepper for taking pictures of me. Every day, it turns out, is a bad hair day.

My heartfelt gratitude to Todd Swift, Stephanie Bolster, Rob Allen and Steve Luxton for their careful readings, opinions (but not "Suggestions and Guidelines") and generous support, and to Jon Paul Fiorentino for resurrecting the title controversy at the last possible moment. Special thanks to David McGimpsey for his friendship, his meticulous eye (and ear), and for all the enlightening poetry talk.

My love and thanks to Irving & Sylvia, Gayle & Robert, Julia, and the rest of my amazing family, and to Ad, Moti (Matt R.) & Arj, all key sources of support and inspiration.

This book is dedicated to the loves of my life: Cory, Oscy and Nava.

Jason Camlot is a poet, songwriter and scholar. His previous poetry collections include, *The Animal Library* (DC Books, 2000), and a limited edition chapbook with illustrations by Canadian artist Betty Goodwin, entitled, *Lines Crossed Out* (Delirium Press, 2005). He received his Ph.D. from Stanford University, and currently teaches Victorian literature at Concordia University in Montreal.